THE BJJ

BRAZILIAN JIU JITSU

TRAINING

DIARY

WRITTEN BY

COREY LILLIS

BJJ Club & Tournament Fundraisers
Bulk orders of *The BJJ Training Diary* can be arranged
for club and tournament fundraisers.

Advertisements
If you are interested in advertising in
The BJJ Training Diary,
please contact **coreylillis@gmail.com**.

How to Use The BJJ Training Diary

In this book you will find the following sections:
- Daily Drill Guide,
- Daily Training Journal, and
- Tournament Results, and
- IBJJF Gi and No Gi Weight Divisions

To get the best results when using *The BJJ Training Diary,* consider following the suggestions outlined below.

1. **Three Training Goals:** On the days that you train, make sure you pick three training goals prior to class. This will bring clarity to each training session. For example, I might want to ask my instructor to clarify a specific position that I am having difficulty with, or I may want to work on a particular pass when rolling, or spend some time working a specific sweep.

2. **Record Pre Workout Meal:** Record the meals and your response to them. This allows you to learn what combination of foods or meals provide you with the best fuel. This can be extremely helpful to know when planning a meal on competition days.

3. **Hydration:** We need water to perform and recover optimally. Our hydration needs are often overlooked, causing us other issues so take time to document this throughout the day.

4. **Drills:** After class, record the drills that you were working on in class. Remember repetition builds muscle memory. If you are unsure of how to perform a specific drill record this in the drill comments to refer back to at a later time.

5. **Techniques:** After class, record the technique or techniques that were taught, as well as, the proper steps for performing the technique. We all tend to forget a key part of the technique days or weeks after. Having the steps there to refer back to will help you immensely.

6. **Notes:** On the page training notes, record any info from the class that you may want to remember, such as questions and what I like to call Rolling Reflections. Did you get caught in any submissions? Record what they were. Did you get your guard passed? What techniques were used? By analyzing your reflections, you can dramatically improve your game.

7. **Tournament:** In the Tournament Results section try to record as much info about your matches as possible. The BJJ community is small so the chance to compete against your opponent again is very common. These notes can provide info on what you need to focus on when back at class, as well as, what you need to do when prepping for a similar opponent.

DRILL CHALLENGES

These can be done solo, or with a partner, before or after class.
Drills, courtesy of Roberto Atalla, can be found at these links:
http://tinyurl.com/7drills
http://tinyurl.com/7dailydrills

DRILLS:

Front and Back Rolls
Side Rolls
Technical Stand-Up
Hip Escapes
Bridge and Hip Escape Combo
Hip Switch
Bridge and Mount Escape

Technique Notes

PARTNER DRILLS (to improve your guard):

Guard Pumbling

Guard Recovery Using Hips

Guard Recovery from North/South

Guard Recovery Using Shoulders

Arm Bar Drill from Guard

Open Guard Triangle Drill

Technique Notes

DAILY TRAINING JOURNAL

Date:	Coach:
Daily Goals	Completed
1.	☐ Yes ☐ No ☐ Needs Improvement
2.	☐ Yes ☐ No ☐ Needs Improvement
3.	☐ Yes ☐ No ☐ Needs Improvement
Pre workout meal:	
Daily water intake (glasses)	☐ ☐ ☐ ☐ ☐ ☐ ☐ ☐ ☐ ☐ ☐ ☐ ☐ ☐ ☐ ☐
Daily Drills	Drill Comments
Daily Techniques	Technique Comments

Training Notes:

Date:	Coach:
Daily Goals	Completed
1.	☐ Yes ☐ No ☐ Needs Improvement
2.	☐ Yes ☐ No ☐ Needs Improvement
3.	☐ Yes ☐ No ☐ Needs Improvement
Pre workout meal:	
Daily water intake (glasses)	☐ ☐ ☐ ☐ ☐ ☐ ☐ ☐ ☐ ☐ ☐ ☐ ☐ ☐ ☐ ☐
Daily Drills	Drill Comments
Daily Techniques	Technique Comments

MY BJJ TRAINING DIARY

Training Notes:

Date:	Coach:
Daily Goals	Completed
1.	☐ Yes ☐ No ☐ Needs Improvement
2.	☐ Yes ☐ No ☐ Needs Improvement
3.	☐ Yes ☐ No ☐ Needs Improvement
Pre workout meal:	
Daily water intake (glasses)	☐ ☐ ☐ ☐ ☐ ☐ ☐ ☐ ☐ ☐ ☐ ☐ ☐ ☐ ☐ ☐
Daily Drills	Drill Comments
Daily Techniques	Technique Comments

Training Notes:

Date:	Coach:
Daily Goals	Completed
1.	☐ Yes ☐ No ☐ Needs Improvement
2.	☐ Yes ☐ No ☐ Needs Improvement
3.	☐ Yes ☐ No ☐ Needs Improvement
Pre workout meal:	
Daily water intake (glasses)	☐ ☐ ☐ ☐ ☐ ☐ ☐ ☐ ☐ ☐ ☐ ☐ ☐ ☐ ☐ ☐
Daily Drills	Drill Comments
Daily Techniques	Technique Comments

Training Notes:

Date:	Coach:
Daily Goals	Completed
1.	☐ Yes ☐ No ☐ Needs Improvement
2.	☐ Yes ☐ No ☐ Needs Improvement
3.	☐ Yes ☐ No ☐ Needs Improvement
Pre workout meal:	
Daily water intake (glasses)	☐ ☐ ☐ ☐ ☐ ☐ ☐ ☐ ☐ ☐ ☐ ☐ ☐ ☐ ☐ ☐
Daily Drills	Drill Comments
Daily Techniques	Technique Comments

Training Notes:

Date:	Coach:
Daily Goals	Completed
1.	☐ Yes ☐ No ☐ Needs Improvement
2.	☐ Yes ☐ No ☐ Needs Improvement
3.	☐ Yes ☐ No ☐ Needs Improvement
Pre workout meal:	
Daily water intake (glasses)	☐ ☐ ☐ ☐ ☐ ☐ ☐ ☐ ☐ ☐ ☐ ☐ ☐ ☐ ☐ ☐
Daily Drills	Drill Comments
Daily Techniques	Technique Comments

Training Notes:

Date:	Coach:
Daily Goals	Completed
1.	☐ Yes ☐ No ☐ Needs Improvement
2.	☐ Yes ☐ No ☐ Needs Improvement
3.	☐ Yes ☐ No ☐ Needs Improvement
Pre workout meal:	
Daily water intake (glasses)	☐ ☐ ☐ ☐ ☐ ☐ ☐ ☐ ☐ ☐ ☐ ☐ ☐ ☐ ☐ ☐
Daily Drills	Drill Comments
Daily Techniques	Technique Comments

Training Notes:

MY BJJ TRAINING DIARY

Date:	Coach:
Daily Goals	Completed
1.	☐ Yes ☐ No ☐ Needs Improvement
2.	☐ Yes ☐ No ☐ Needs Improvement
3.	☐ Yes ☐ No ☐ Needs Improvement
Pre workout meal:	
Daily water intake (glasses)	☐ ☐ ☐ ☐ ☐ ☐ ☐ ☐ ☐ ☐ ☐ ☐ ☐ ☐ ☐ ☐
Daily Drills	Drill Comments
Daily Techniques	Technique Comments

COREY LILLIS | www.coreylillis.com

Training Notes:

Date:	Coach:
Daily Goals	Completed
1.	☐ Yes ☐ No ☐ Needs Improvement
2.	☐ Yes ☐ No ☐ Needs Improvement
3.	☐ Yes ☐ No ☐ Needs Improvement
Pre workout meal:	
Daily water intake (glasses)	☐ ☐ ☐ ☐ ☐ ☐ ☐ ☐ ☐ ☐ ☐ ☐ ☐ ☐ ☐ ☐
Daily Drills	Drill Comments
Daily Techniques	Technique Comments

Training Notes:

Date:	Coach:
Daily Goals	Completed
1.	☐ Yes ☐ No ☐ Needs Improvement
2.	☐ Yes ☐ No ☐ Needs Improvement
3.	☐ Yes ☐ No ☐ Needs Improvement
Pre workout meal:	
Daily water intake (glasses)	☐ ☐ ☐ ☐ ☐ ☐ ☐ ☐ ☐ ☐ ☐ ☐ ☐ ☐ ☐ ☐
Daily Drills	Drill Comments
Daily Techniques	Technique Comments

Training Notes:

Date:	Coach:
Daily Goals	Completed
1.	☐ Yes ☐ No ☐ Needs Improvement
2.	☐ Yes ☐ No ☐ Needs Improvement
3.	☐ Yes ☐ No ☐ Needs Improvement
Pre workout meal:	
Daily water intake (glasses)	☐ ☐ ☐ ☐ ☐ ☐ ☐ ☐ ☐ ☐ ☐ ☐ ☐ ☐ ☐ ☐
Daily Drills	Drill Comments
Daily Techniques	Technique Comments

Training Notes:

Date:	Coach:
Daily Goals	Completed
1.	☐ Yes ☐ No ☐ Needs Improvement
2.	☐ Yes ☐ No ☐ Needs Improvement
3.	☐ Yes ☐ No ☐ Needs Improvement
Pre workout meal:	
Daily water intake (glasses)	☐ ☐ ☐ ☐ ☐ ☐ ☐ ☐ ☐ ☐ ☐ ☐ ☐ ☐ ☐ ☐
Daily Drills	Drill Comments
Daily Techniques	Technique Comments

Training Notes:

Date:	**Coach:**
Daily Goals	Completed
1.	☐ Yes ☐ No ☐ Needs Improvement
2.	☐ Yes ☐ No ☐ Needs Improvement
3.	☐ Yes ☐ No ☐ Needs Improvement
Pre workout meal:	
Daily water intake (glasses)	☐ ☐ ☐ ☐ ☐ ☐ ☐ ☐ ☐ ☐ ☐ ☐ ☐ ☐ ☐ ☐
Daily Drills	Drill Comments
Daily Techniques	Technique Comments

Training Notes:

Date:	Coach:
Daily Goals	Completed
1.	☐ Yes ☐ No ☐ Needs Improvement
2.	☐ Yes ☐ No ☐ Needs Improvement
3.	☐ Yes ☐ No ☐ Needs Improvement
Pre workout meal:	
Daily water intake (glasses)	☐ ☐ ☐ ☐ ☐ ☐ ☐ ☐ ☐ ☐ ☐ ☐ ☐ ☐ ☐ ☐
Daily Drills	Drill Comments
Daily Techniques	Technique Comments

Training Notes:

Date:	Coach:
Daily Goals	Completed
1.	☐ Yes ☐ No ☐ Needs Improvement
2.	☐ Yes ☐ No ☐ Needs Improvement
3.	☐ Yes ☐ No ☐ Needs Improvement
Pre workout meal:	
Daily water intake (glasses)	☐ ☐ ☐ ☐ ☐ ☐ ☐ ☐ ☐ ☐ ☐ ☐ ☐ ☐ ☐ ☐
Daily Drills	Drill Comments
Daily Techniques	Technique Comments

Training Notes:

Date:	**Coach:**
Daily Goals	Completed
1.	☐ Yes ☐ No ☐ Needs Improvement
2.	☐ Yes ☐ No ☐ Needs Improvement
3.	☐ Yes ☐ No ☐ Needs Improvement
Pre workout meal:	
Daily water intake (glasses)	☐ ☐ ☐ ☐ ☐ ☐ ☐ ☐ ☐ ☐ ☐ ☐ ☐ ☐ ☐ ☐
Daily Drills	Drill Comments
Daily Techniques	Technique Comments

MY BJJ TRAINING DIARY

Training Notes:

Date:	Coach:
Daily Goals	Completed
1.	☐ Yes ☐ No ☐ Needs Improvement
2.	☐ Yes ☐ No ☐ Needs Improvement
3.	☐ Yes ☐ No ☐ Needs Improvement
Pre workout meal:	
Daily water intake (glasses)	☐ ☐ ☐ ☐ ☐ ☐ ☐ ☐ ☐ ☐ ☐ ☐ ☐ ☐ ☐ ☐
Daily Drills	Drill Comments
Daily Techniques	Technique Comments

Training Notes:

Date:	Coach:
Daily Goals	Completed
1.	☐ Yes ☐ No ☐ Needs Improvement
2.	☐ Yes ☐ No ☐ Needs Improvement
3.	☐ Yes ☐ No ☐ Needs Improvement
Pre workout meal:	
Daily water intake (glasses)	☐ ☐ ☐ ☐ ☐ ☐ ☐ ☐ ☐ ☐ ☐ ☐ ☐ ☐ ☐ ☐
Daily Drills	Drill Comments
Daily Techniques	Technique Comments

Training Notes:

Date:	Coach:
Daily Goals	Completed
1.	☐ Yes ☐ No ☐ Needs Improvement
2.	☐ Yes ☐ No ☐ Needs Improvement
3.	☐ Yes ☐ No ☐ Needs Improvement
Pre workout meal:	
Daily water intake (glasses)	☐ ☐ ☐ ☐ ☐ ☐ ☐ ☐ ☐ ☐ ☐ ☐ ☐ ☐ ☐ ☐
Daily Drills	Drill Comments
Daily Techniques	Technique Comments

Training Notes:

Date:	Coach:
Daily Goals	Completed
1.	☐ Yes ☐ No ☐ Needs Improvement
2.	☐ Yes ☐ No ☐ Needs Improvement
3.	☐ Yes ☐ No ☐ Needs Improvement
Pre workout meal:	
Daily water intake (glasses)	☐ ☐ ☐ ☐ ☐ ☐ ☐ ☐ ☐ ☐ ☐ ☐ ☐ ☐ ☐ ☐
Daily Drills	Drill Comments
Daily Techniques	Technique Comments

Training Notes:

Date:	Coach:
Daily Goals	Completed
1.	☐ Yes ☐ No ☐ Needs Improvement
2.	☐ Yes ☐ No ☐ Needs Improvement
3.	☐ Yes ☐ No ☐ Needs Improvement
Pre workout meal:	
Daily water intake (glasses)	☐ ☐ ☐ ☐ ☐ ☐ ☐ ☐ ☐ ☐ ☐ ☐ ☐ ☐ ☐ ☐
Daily Drills	Drill Comments
Daily Techniques	Technique Comments

Training Notes:

Date:	Coach:
Daily Goals	Completed
1.	☐ Yes ☐ No ☐ Needs Improvement
2.	☐ Yes ☐ No ☐ Needs Improvement
3.	☐ Yes ☐ No ☐ Needs Improvement
Pre workout meal:	
Daily water intake (glasses)	☐ ☐ ☐ ☐ ☐ ☐ ☐ ☐ ☐ ☐ ☐ ☐ ☐ ☐ ☐ ☐
Daily Drills	Drill Comments
Daily Techniques	Technique Comments

Training Notes:

Date:	Coach:
Daily Goals	Completed
1.	☐ Yes ☐ No ☐ Needs Improvement
2.	☐ Yes ☐ No ☐ Needs Improvement
3.	☐ Yes ☐ No ☐ Needs Improvement
Pre workout meal:	
Daily water intake (glasses)	☐ ☐ ☐ ☐ ☐ ☐ ☐ ☐ ☐ ☐ ☐ ☐ ☐ ☐ ☐ ☐
Daily Drills	Drill Comments
Daily Techniques	Technique Comments

Training Notes:

Date:	Coach:
Daily Goals	Completed
1.	☐ Yes ☐ No ☐ Needs Improvement
2.	☐ Yes ☐ No ☐ Needs Improvement
3.	☐ Yes ☐ No ☐ Needs Improvement
Pre workout meal:	
Daily water intake (glasses)	☐ ☐ ☐ ☐ ☐ ☐ ☐ ☐ ☐ ☐ ☐ ☐ ☐ ☐ ☐ ☐
Daily Drills	Drill Comments
Daily Techniques	Technique Comments

Training Notes:

Date:	Coach:
Daily Goals	Completed
1.	☐ Yes ☐ No ☐ Needs Improvement
2.	☐ Yes ☐ No ☐ Needs Improvement
3.	☐ Yes ☐ No ☐ Needs Improvement
Pre workout meal:	
Daily water intake (glasses)	☐ ☐ ☐ ☐ ☐ ☐ ☐ ☐ ☐ ☐ ☐ ☐ ☐ ☐ ☐ ☐
Daily Drills	Drill Comments
Daily Techniques	Technique Comments

Training Notes:

Date:	Coach:
Daily Goals	Completed
1.	☐ Yes ☐ No ☐ Needs Improvement
2.	☐ Yes ☐ No ☐ Needs Improvement
3.	☐ Yes ☐ No ☐ Needs Improvement
Pre workout meal:	
Daily water intake (glasses)	☐ ☐ ☐ ☐ ☐ ☐ ☐ ☐ ☐ ☐ ☐ ☐ ☐ ☐ ☐ ☐
Daily Drills	Drill Comments
Daily Techniques	Technique Comments

Training Notes:

Date:	Coach:
Daily Goals	Completed
1.	☐ Yes ☐ No ☐ Needs Improvement
2.	☐ Yes ☐ No ☐ Needs Improvement
3.	☐ Yes ☐ No ☐ Needs Improvement
Pre workout meal:	
Daily water intake (glasses)	☐ ☐ ☐ ☐ ☐ ☐ ☐ ☐ ☐ ☐ ☐ ☐ ☐ ☐ ☐ ☐
Daily Drills	Drill Comments
Daily Techniques	Technique Comments

Training Notes:

Date:	Coach:
Daily Goals	Completed
1.	☐ Yes ☐ No ☐ Needs Improvement
2.	☐ Yes ☐ No ☐ Needs Improvement
3.	☐ Yes ☐ No ☐ Needs Improvement
Pre workout meal:	
Daily water intake (glasses)	☐ ☐ ☐ ☐ ☐ ☐ ☐ ☐ ☐ ☐ ☐ ☐ ☐ ☐ ☐ ☐
Daily Drills	Drill Comments
Daily Techniques	Technique Comments

Training Notes:

Date:	**Coach:**
Daily Goals	Completed
1.	☐ Yes ☐ No ☐ Needs Improvement
2.	☐ Yes ☐ No ☐ Needs Improvement
3.	☐ Yes ☐ No ☐ Needs Improvement
Pre workout meal:	
Daily water intake (glasses)	☐ ☐ ☐ ☐ ☐ ☐ ☐ ☐ ☐ ☐ ☐ ☐ ☐ ☐ ☐ ☐
Daily Drills	Drill Comments
Daily Techniques	Technique Comments

Training Notes:

MY BJJ TRAINING DIARY

Date:	Coach:
Daily Goals	Completed
1.	☐ Yes ☐ No ☐ Needs Improvement
2.	☐ Yes ☐ No ☐ Needs Improvement
3.	☐ Yes ☐ No ☐ Needs Improvement
Pre workout meal:	
Daily water intake (glasses)	☐ ☐ ☐ ☐ ☐ ☐ ☐ ☐ ☐ ☐ ☐ ☐ ☐ ☐ ☐
Daily Drills	Drill Comments
Daily Techniques	Technique Comments

COREY LILLIS | www.coreylillis.com

Training Notes:

Date:	Coach:
Daily Goals	Completed
1.	☐ Yes ☐ No ☐ Needs Improvement
2.	☐ Yes ☐ No ☐ Needs Improvement
3.	☐ Yes ☐ No ☐ Needs Improvement
Pre workout meal:	
Daily water intake (glasses)	☐ ☐ ☐ ☐ ☐ ☐ ☐ ☐ ☐ ☐ ☐ ☐ ☐ ☐ ☐ ☐
Daily Drills	Drill Comments
Daily Techniques	Technique Comments

Training Notes:

Date:	Coach:
Daily Goals	Completed
1.	☐ Yes ☐ No ☐ Needs Improvement
2.	☐ Yes ☐ No ☐ Needs Improvement
3.	☐ Yes ☐ No ☐ Needs Improvement
Pre workout meal:	
Daily water intake (glasses)	☐ ☐ ☐ ☐ ☐ ☐ ☐ ☐ ☐ ☐ ☐ ☐ ☐ ☐ ☐ ☐
Daily Drills	Drill Comments
Daily Techniques	Technique Comments

Training Notes:

Date:	Coach:
Daily Goals	Completed
1.	☐ Yes ☐ No ☐ Needs Improvement
2.	☐ Yes ☐ No ☐ Needs Improvement
3.	☐ Yes ☐ No ☐ Needs Improvement
Pre workout meal:	
Daily water intake (glasses)	☐ ☐ ☐ ☐ ☐ ☐ ☐ ☐ ☐ ☐ ☐ ☐ ☐ ☐ ☐ ☐
Daily Drills	Drill Comments
Daily Techniques	Technique Comments

Training Notes:

Date:	Coach:
Daily Goals	Completed
1.	☐ Yes ☐ No ☐ Needs Improvement
2.	☐ Yes ☐ No ☐ Needs Improvement
3.	☐ Yes ☐ No ☐ Needs Improvement
Pre workout meal:	
Daily water intake (glasses)	☐ ☐ ☐ ☐ ☐ ☐ ☐ ☐ ☐ ☐ ☐ ☐ ☐ ☐ ☐ ☐
Daily Drills	Drill Comments
Daily Techniques	Technique Comments

Training Notes:

Date:	Coach:
Daily Goals	Completed
1.	☐ Yes ☐ No ☐ Needs Improvement
2.	☐ Yes ☐ No ☐ Needs Improvement
3.	☐ Yes ☐ No ☐ Needs Improvement
Pre workout meal:	
Daily water intake (glasses)	☐ ☐ ☐ ☐ ☐ ☐ ☐ ☐ ☐ ☐ ☐ ☐ ☐ ☐ ☐ ☐
Daily Drills	Drill Comments
Daily Techniques	Technique Comments

Training Notes:

Date:	Coach:
Daily Goals	Completed
1.	☐ Yes ☐ No ☐ Needs Improvement
2.	☐ Yes ☐ No ☐ Needs Improvement
3.	☐ Yes ☐ No ☐ Needs Improvement
Pre workout meal:	
Daily water intake (glasses)	☐ ☐ ☐ ☐ ☐ ☐ ☐ ☐ ☐ ☐ ☐ ☐ ☐ ☐ ☐ ☐
Daily Drills	Drill Comments
Daily Techniques	Technique Comments

Training Notes:

Date:	Coach:
Daily Goals	Completed
1.	☐ Yes ☐ No ☐ Needs Improvement
2.	☐ Yes ☐ No ☐ Needs Improvement
3.	☐ Yes ☐ No ☐ Needs Improvement
Pre workout meal:	
Daily water intake (glasses)	☐ ☐ ☐ ☐ ☐ ☐ ☐ ☐ ☐ ☐ ☐ ☐ ☐ ☐ ☐ ☐
Daily Drills	Drill Comments
Daily Techniques	Technique Comments

Training Notes:

Date:	Coach:
Daily Goals	Completed
1.	☐ Yes ☐ No ☐ Needs Improvement
2.	☐ Yes ☐ No ☐ Needs Improvement
3.	☐ Yes ☐ No ☐ Needs Improvement
Pre workout meal:	
Daily water intake (glasses)	☐ ☐ ☐ ☐ ☐ ☐ ☐ ☐ ☐ ☐ ☐ ☐ ☐ ☐ ☐ ☐
Daily Drills	Drill Comments
Daily Techniques	Technique Comments

Training Notes:

Date:	**Coach:**
Daily Goals	Completed
1.	☐ Yes ☐ No ☐ Needs Improvement
2.	☐ Yes ☐ No ☐ Needs Improvement
3.	☐ Yes ☐ No ☐ Needs Improvement
Pre workout meal:	
Daily water intake (glasses)	☐ ☐ ☐ ☐ ☐ ☐ ☐ ☐ ☐ ☐ ☐ ☐ ☐ ☐ ☐ ☐
Daily Drills	Drill Comments
Daily Techniques	Technique Comments

MY BJJ TRAINING DIARY

Training Notes:

Date:	Coach:
Daily Goals	Completed
1.	☐ Yes ☐ No ☐ Needs Improvement
2.	☐ Yes ☐ No ☐ Needs Improvement
3.	☐ Yes ☐ No ☐ Needs Improvement
Pre workout meal:	
Daily water intake (glasses)	☐ ☐ ☐ ☐ ☐ ☐ ☐ ☐ ☐ ☐ ☐ ☐ ☐ ☐ ☐ ☐
Daily Drills	Drill Comments
Daily Techniques	Technique Comments

Training Notes:

Date:	Coach:
Daily Goals	Completed
1.	☐ Yes ☐ No ☐ Needs Improvement
2.	☐ Yes ☐ No ☐ Needs Improvement
3.	☐ Yes ☐ No ☐ Needs Improvement
Pre workout meal:	
Daily water intake (glasses)	☐ ☐ ☐ ☐ ☐ ☐ ☐ ☐ ☐ ☐ ☐ ☐ ☐ ☐ ☐ ☐
Daily Drills	Drill Comments
Daily Techniques	Technique Comments

Training Notes:

Date:	Coach:
Daily Goals	Completed
1.	☐ Yes ☐ No ☐ Needs Improvement
2.	☐ Yes ☐ No ☐ Needs Improvement
3.	☐ Yes ☐ No ☐ Needs Improvement
Pre workout meal:	
Daily water intake (glasses)	☐ ☐ ☐ ☐ ☐ ☐ ☐ ☐ ☐ ☐ ☐ ☐ ☐ ☐ ☐ ☐
Daily Drills	Drill Comments
Daily Techniques	Technique Comments

Training Notes:

Date:	Coach:
Daily Goals	Completed
1.	☐ Yes ☐ No ☐ Needs Improvement
2.	☐ Yes ☐ No ☐ Needs Improvement
3.	☐ Yes ☐ No ☐ Needs Improvement
Pre workout meal:	
Daily water intake (glasses)	☐ ☐ ☐ ☐ ☐ ☐ ☐ ☐ ☐ ☐ ☐ ☐ ☐ ☐ ☐ ☐
Daily Drills	Drill Comments
Daily Techniques	Technique Comments

Training Notes:

Date:	Coach:		
Daily Goals	Completed		
1.	☐ Yes ☐ No ☐ Needs Improvement		
2.	☐ Yes ☐ No ☐ Needs Improvement		
3.	☐ Yes ☐ No ☐ Needs Improvement		
Pre workout meal:			
Daily water intake (glasses)	☐ ☐ ☐ ☐ ☐ ☐ ☐ ☐ ☐ ☐ ☐ ☐ ☐ ☐ ☐ ☐		
Daily Drills	Drill Comments		
Daily Techniques	Technique Comments		

Training Notes:

Date:	Coach:
Daily Goals	Completed
1.	☐ Yes ☐ No ☐ Needs Improvement
2.	☐ Yes ☐ No ☐ Needs Improvement
3.	☐ Yes ☐ No ☐ Needs Improvement
Pre workout meal:	
Daily water intake (glasses)	☐ ☐ ☐ ☐ ☐ ☐ ☐ ☐ ☐ ☐ ☐ ☐ ☐ ☐ ☐ ☐
Daily Drills	Drill Comments
Daily Techniques	Technique Comments

Training Notes:

Date:	Coach:
Daily Goals	Completed
1.	☐ Yes ☐ No ☐ Needs Improvement
2.	☐ Yes ☐ No ☐ Needs Improvement
3.	☐ Yes ☐ No ☐ Needs Improvement
Pre workout meal:	
Daily water intake (glasses)	☐ ☐ ☐ ☐ ☐ ☐ ☐ ☐ ☐ ☐ ☐ ☐ ☐ ☐ ☐ ☐
Daily Drills	Drill Comments
Daily Techniques	Technique Comments

Training Notes:

Date:	Coach:
Daily Goals	Completed
1.	☐ Yes ☐ No ☐ Needs Improvement
2.	☐ Yes ☐ No ☐ Needs Improvement
3.	☐ Yes ☐ No ☐ Needs Improvement
Pre workout meal:	
Daily water intake (glasses)	☐ ☐ ☐ ☐ ☐ ☐ ☐ ☐ ☐ ☐ ☐ ☐ ☐ ☐ ☐ ☐
Daily Drills	Drill Comments
Daily Techniques	Technique Comments

Training Notes:

Date:	Coach:
Daily Goals	Completed
1.	☐ Yes ☐ No ☐ Needs Improvement
2.	☐ Yes ☐ No ☐ Needs Improvement
3.	☐ Yes ☐ No ☐ Needs Improvement
Pre workout meal:	
Daily water intake (glasses)	☐ ☐ ☐ ☐ ☐ ☐ ☐ ☐ ☐ ☐ ☐ ☐ ☐ ☐ ☐ ☐
Daily Drills	Drill Comments
Daily Techniques	Technique Comments

Training Notes:

Date:	Coach:
Daily Goals	Completed
1.	☐ Yes ☐ No ☐ Needs Improvement
2.	☐ Yes ☐ No ☐ Needs Improvement
3.	☐ Yes ☐ No ☐ Needs Improvement
Pre workout meal:	
Daily water intake (glasses)	☐ ☐ ☐ ☐ ☐ ☐ ☐ ☐ ☐ ☐ ☐ ☐ ☐ ☐ ☐ ☐
Daily Drills	Drill Comments
Daily Techniques	Technique Comments

Training Notes:

Date:	Coach:
Daily Goals	Completed
1.	☐ Yes ☐ No ☐ Needs Improvement
2.	☐ Yes ☐ No ☐ Needs Improvement
3.	☐ Yes ☐ No ☐ Needs Improvement
Pre workout meal:	
Daily water intake (glasses)	☐ ☐ ☐ ☐ ☐ ☐ ☐ ☐ ☐ ☐ ☐ ☐ ☐ ☐ ☐ ☐
Daily Drills	Drill Comments
Daily Techniques	Technique Comments

Training Notes:

Date:	Coach:
Daily Goals	Completed
1.	☐ Yes ☐ No ☐ Needs Improvement
2.	☐ Yes ☐ No ☐ Needs Improvement
3.	☐ Yes ☐ No ☐ Needs Improvement
Pre workout meal:	
Daily water intake (glasses)	☐ ☐ ☐ ☐ ☐ ☐ ☐ ☐ ☐ ☐ ☐ ☐ ☐ ☐ ☐ ☐
Daily Drills	Drill Comments
Daily Techniques	Technique Comments

Training Notes:

Date:	**Coach:**
Daily Goals	Completed
1.	☐ Yes ☐ No ☐ Needs Improvement
2.	☐ Yes ☐ No ☐ Needs Improvement
3.	☐ Yes ☐ No ☐ Needs Improvement
Pre workout meal:	
Daily water intake (glasses)	☐ ☐ ☐ ☐ ☐ ☐ ☐ ☐ ☐ ☐ ☐ ☐ ☐ ☐ ☐ ☐
Daily Drills	Drill Comments
Daily Techniques	Technique Comments

Training Notes:

TOURNAMENT RESULTS

Date:	Number of Matches:

OPPONENT:

	☐ Win	☐ Loss

MATCH NOTES:

OPPONENT:

	☐ Win	☐ Loss

MATCH NOTES:

OPPONENT:

	☐ Win	☐ Loss

MATCH NOTES:

Date:	Number of Matches:

OPPONENT:

	☐ Win	☐ Loss

MATCH NOTES:

\
\
\
\
\
\
\
\
\
\
\

OPPONENT:

	☐ Win	☐ Loss

MATCH NOTES:

\
\
\
\
\
\
\
\

OPPONENT:

	☐ Win	☐ Loss

MATCH NOTES:

\
\
\
\
\
\
\
\

General Tournament Reflection

Technique Notes

Date:	Number of Matches:

OPPONENT:

☐ Win   ☐ Loss

MATCH NOTES:

OPPONENT:

☐ Win   ☐ Loss

MATCH NOTES:

OPPONENT:

☐ Win   ☐ Loss

MATCH NOTES:

Date:	Number of Matches:

OPPONENT:		
	☐ Win	☐ Loss

MATCH NOTES:

_____

_____

_____

_____

_____

_____

_____

_____

_____

_____

OPPONENT:		
	☐ Win	☐ Loss

MATCH NOTES:

_____

_____

_____

_____

_____

_____

_____

_____

OPPONENT:		
	☐ Win	☐ Loss

MATCH NOTES:

_____

_____

_____

_____

_____

_____

_____

_____

General Tournament Reflection

Technique Notes

Date:	Number of Matches:

OPPONENT:

	☐ Win	☐ Loss

MATCH NOTES:

OPPONENT:

	☐ Win	☐ Loss

MATCH NOTES:

OPPONENT:

	☐ Win	☐ Loss

MATCH NOTES:

Date:	Number of Matches:

OPPONENT:

☐ Win   ☐ Loss

MATCH NOTES:

_____
_____
_____
_____
_____
_____
_____
_____
_____
_____

OPPONENT:

☐ Win   ☐ Loss

MATCH NOTES:

_____
_____
_____
_____
_____
_____
_____
_____

OPPONENT:

☐ Win   ☐ Loss

MATCH NOTES:

_____
_____
_____
_____
_____
_____
_____
_____

General Tournament Reflection

Technique Notes

Date:	Number of Matches:

OPPONENT:

	☐ Win	☐ Loss

MATCH NOTES:

_____
_____
_____
_____
_____
_____
_____
_____
_____
_____

OPPONENT:

	☐ Win	☐ Loss

MATCH NOTES:

_____
_____
_____
_____
_____
_____
_____
_____

OPPONENT:

	☐ Win	☐ Loss

MATCH NOTES:

_____
_____
_____
_____
_____
_____
_____
_____

Date:	Number of Matches:

OPPONENT:

	☐ Win	☐ Loss

MATCH NOTES:

OPPONENT:

	☐ Win	☐ Loss

MATCH NOTES:

OPPONENT:

	☐ Win	☐ Loss

MATCH NOTES:

General Tournament Reflection

Technique Notes

Date:	Number of Matches:

OPPONENT:

☐ Win   ☐ Loss

MATCH NOTES:

OPPONENT:

☐ Win   ☐ Loss

MATCH NOTES:

OPPONENT:

☐ Win   ☐ Loss

MATCH NOTES:

Date:	Number of Matches:

OPPONENT:

	☐ Win ☐ Loss

MATCH NOTES:

_____
_____
_____
_____
_____
_____
_____
_____
_____
_____

OPPONENT:

	☐ Win ☐ Loss

MATCH NOTES:

_____
_____
_____
_____
_____
_____
_____
_____

OPPONENT:

	☐ Win ☐ Loss

MATCH NOTES:

_____
_____
_____
_____
_____
_____
_____
_____

MY BJJ TRAINING DIARY

General Tournament Reflection

COREY LILLIS | www.coreylillis.com

Technique Notes

Date:	Number of Matches:

OPPONENT:

	☐ Win ☐ Loss

MATCH NOTES:

_____

_____

_____

_____

_____

_____

_____

_____

_____

_____

OPPONENT:

	☐ Win ☐ Loss

MATCH NOTES:

_____

_____

_____

_____

_____

_____

_____

_____

_____

OPPONENT:

	☐ Win ☐ Loss

MATCH NOTES:

_____

_____

_____

_____

_____

_____

_____

_____

_____

Date:	Number of Matches:

OPPONENT:

	☐ Win	☐ Loss

MATCH NOTES:

_____
_____
_____
_____
_____
_____
_____
_____
_____
_____
_____

OPPONENT:

	☐ Win	☐ Loss

MATCH NOTES:

_____
_____
_____
_____
_____
_____
_____
_____
_____

OPPONENT:

	☐ Win	☐ Loss

MATCH NOTES:

_____
_____
_____
_____
_____
_____
_____
_____
_____

General Tournament Reflection

Technique Notes

Date:	Number of Matches:

OPPONENT:

	☐ Win	☐ Loss

MATCH NOTES:

OPPONENT:

	☐ Win	☐ Loss

MATCH NOTES:

OPPONENT:

	☐ Win	☐ Loss

MATCH NOTES:

Date:	Number of Matches:

OPPONENT:

	☐ Win	☐ Loss

MATCH NOTES:

_____

_____

_____

_____

_____

_____

_____

_____

_____

_____

_____

OPPONENT:

	☐ Win	☐ Loss

MATCH NOTES:

_____

_____

_____

_____

_____

_____

_____

_____

OPPONENT:

	☐ Win	☐ Loss

MATCH NOTES:

_____

_____

_____

_____

_____

_____

_____

_____

_____

General Tournament Reflection

Technique Notes

Date:	Number of Matches:

OPPONENT:

	☐ Win	☐ Loss

MATCH NOTES:

OPPONENT:

	☐ Win	☐ Loss

MATCH NOTES:

OPPONENT:

	☐ Win	☐ Loss

MATCH NOTES:

Date:	Number of Matches:

OPPONENT:

☐ Win	☐ Loss

MATCH NOTES:

_____
_____
_____
_____
_____
_____
_____
_____
_____
_____
_____

OPPONENT:

☐ Win	☐ Loss

MATCH NOTES:

_____
_____
_____
_____
_____
_____
_____
_____

OPPONENT:

☐ Win	☐ Loss

MATCH NOTES:

_____
_____
_____
_____
_____
_____
_____
_____
_____

General Tournament Reflection

Technique Notes

Date:	Number of Matches:

OPPONENT:

	☐ Win	☐ Loss

MATCH NOTES:

OPPONENT:

	☐ Win	☐ Loss

MATCH NOTES:

OPPONENT:

	☐ Win	☐ Loss

MATCH NOTES:

Date:	Number of Matches:

OPPONENT:

☐ Win   ☐ Loss

MATCH NOTES:

_____
_____
_____
_____
_____
_____
_____
_____
_____
_____

OPPONENT:

☐ Win   ☐ Loss

MATCH NOTES:

_____
_____
_____
_____
_____
_____
_____
_____

OPPONENT:

☐ Win   ☐ Loss

MATCH NOTES:

_____
_____
_____
_____
_____
_____
_____

General Tournament Reflection

Technique Notes

Date:	Number of Matches:

OPPONENT:

☐ Win   ☐ Loss

MATCH NOTES:

OPPONENT:

☐ Win   ☐ Loss

MATCH NOTES:

OPPONENT:

☐ Win   ☐ Loss

MATCH NOTES:

Date:	Number of Matches:

OPPONENT:

☐ Win ☐ Loss

MATCH NOTES:

OPPONENT:

☐ Win ☐ Loss

MATCH NOTES:

OPPONENT:

☐ Win ☐ Loss

MATCH NOTES:

General Tournament Reflection

Technique Notes

NO GI WEGHT DIVISION

WEIGHT DIVISIONS			JUVENILE MALE	ADULT, MASTER & SENIOR MALE	ADULT, MASTER & SENIOR MALE	JUVENILE 1 AND 2 FEMALE
ROOSTER GALO	MAXIMUM WEIGHT		114 lbs 51.50 kg	122.5 lbs 55.50 kg		
LIGHT FEATHER PLUMA	MAXIMUM WEIGHT		125 lbs 56.50 kg	136 lbs 61.50 kg	114 lbs 51.50 kg	103 lbs 46.50 kg
FEATHER PENA	MAXIMUM WEIGHT		136 ibs 61.50 kg	149 lbs 67.50 kg	125 lbs 56.50 kg	114 lbs 51.50 kg
LIGHT LEVE	MAXIMUM WEIGHT		147 lbs 66.50 kg	162.5 lbs 73.50 kg	136 ibs 61.50 kg	125 lbs 56.50 kg
MIDDLE MEDIO	MAXIMUM WEIGHT		158 lbs 71.50 kg	175.5 lbs 79.50 kg	147 lbs 66.50 kg	136 ibs 61.50 kg
MEDIUM HEAVY MEIO-PESADO	MAXIMUM WEIGHT		169 lbs 76.50 kg	188.5 lbs 85.50 kg	158 lbs 71.50 kg	147 lbs 66.50 kg
HEAVY PESADO	MAXIMUM WEIGHT		180 lbs 81.50 kg	202 lbs 91.50 kg	No maximum weight	No maximum weight
SUPER HEAVY SUPER PEDSADO	MAXIMUM WEIGHT		191 lbs 86,50 kg	215 lbs 97.50 kg		
ULTRA HEAVY PESADISSIMO	MAXIMUM WEIGHT		No maximum weight	No maximum weight		
OPEN CLASS ABSOLUTO			FREE (middle weight athletes and up are eligible)	FREE	FREE	FREE (middle weight athletes and up are eligible)

GI WEGHT DIVISION

WEIGHT DIVISIONS		JUVENILE 1 MALE	JUVENILE 2 MALE	ADULT, MASTERS MALE	ADULT, MASTER FEMALE	JUVENILE 1 AND 2 FEMALE
ROOSTER GALO	MAXIMUM WEIGHT	107.0 lbs	118.0 lbs	127.0 lbs	107.0lbs	98.0 lbs
LIGHT FEATHER PLUMA	MAXIMUM WEIGHT	118.0 lbs	129.0 lbs	141.5 lbs	118.0 lbs	106.5 lbs
FEATHER PENA	MAXIMUM WEIGHT	129.0 lbs	141.5 lbs	154.5 lbs	129.0 lbs	116.0 lbs
LIGHT LEVE	MAXIMUM WEIGHT	141.0 lbs	152.5 lbs	168.0 lbs	141.5 lbs	125.0 lbs
MIDDLE MEDIO	MAXIMUM WEIGHT	152.0 lbs	163.5 lbs	181.5 lbs	152.5lbs	133.5 lbs
MEDIUM HEAVY MEIO-PESADO	MAXIMUM WEIGHT	163.0 lbs	175.0 lbs	195.0 lbs	163.5 lbs	143.5 lbs
HEAVY PESADO	MAXIMUM WEIGHT	175.0 lbs	186.0 lbs	208.0 lbs	175.0 lbs	152.0 lbs
SUPER HEAVY SUPER PEDSADO	MAXIMUM WEIGHT	186.0 lbs	197.0 lbs	222.0 lbs	No maximum weight	No maximum weight
ULTRA HEAVY PESADISSIMO	MAXIMUM WEIGHT	No maximum weight	No maximum weight	No maximum weight		
OPEN CLASS ABSOLUTO		Middle weight athletes and up		FREE	FREE	Middle weight athletes and up

Make sure you order a new copy of My BJJ Training Diary!